DAY DREAMS IN DIXIE

foreword

If from these verses that I herein present to the public there can spring up within the hearts and minds of my readers even one added thought of love and tenderness for my beloved "Old Southland," or if they can create a greater tolerance for, and comprehension of, this simple, kindly, but much misunderstood Black Folk who for so many years has been our care, then I will feel that the mission of this book has been fulfilled.

THE AUTHOR.

*Dedicated
to
Professor Henry Preston Hughes
Late of Mississippi*

•

ON THE OTHER SIDE

To Professor Henry Preston Hughes, late of Mississippi.

A silent wall between us stands,
 I cannot pierce it through;
The words of grateful love I'd speak
 Can ne'er be heard by you.
The many thoughts I have of you
 My yearning heart must keep;
For I can never reach you more—
 On the other side you sleep.

Your wondrous mind and human heart
 Were spent for such as I,
And in my heart the living flame
 You lit will never die.
To love the good and scorn the vile,
 To fine and worthy be,
To hitch my wagon to a star—
 All this you taught to me.

And when you laid your burdens down
 And wearied fell asleep,
You left so very much of *you*
 For lesser minds to keep.
Through all the years that roll between
 I've held you in my heart,
In every worthy thought or deed
 Your memory played its part.

You sleep beyond the silent wall,
    But can you wake to hear
This message from the heart of one
    You knew in by-gone year?
If I could only make you know
    That in my heart and brain
The ideals set by you have lived
    And you did not strive in vain.

HIS OLE BLACK MAMMY

I'se allus heerd de ole folks tell
  Dat *blood,* hit's thicker'n water,
Meanin' you loves yo' kinfolks best—
  Yo' Maw, an' yo' son and dau'ter.
But I sho' ain't gwine 'gree wid dat,
  'Cause mah bosom's own "pet Lam'my"
Warn't nary a bit of kin ter me—
  I'se jes' his Ole Black Mammy.

Mah little Mistis passed away
  When *he* wuz ten days ole;
She axed me wu'd I keer fer him
  An' treasure him lack gole.
I'd nussed *her* frum a baby, too,
  Back up in Alabammy,
So she knowed I'd sholy tend 'im well
  Ef *I'se* his Ole Black Mammy.

I fed him vittles frum a spoon,
  Slep' on de flo' beside him.
Folks all sed I'd spile 'im so
  Nobody couldn't 'bide him.
I'd walk de floor bofe day an' night,
  'Til mah foots could hardly ca'y me—
Not a livin' soul could tech him, chile,
  But *me,* his Ole Black Mammy.

An' ez he growed up day by day
 He sho' wuz fine and dandy.
I use' ter fry him doughnuts
 An' I'd pull him 'lasses candy;
An' when I'd wash him up at night,
 All garmed an' mussed an' jammy,
He'd hug mah neck and say his prayers
 Ter me, his Ole Black Mammy.

An' when he went away ter school,
 Lawdy, Lawdy, how I missed him;
When he come home fer Chris'mus time,
 I jest grabbed him an' I kissed him.
An' when he went vacation time
 Ter his Maw's folks in Alabammy,
He fetched a *gole* ring home fer me,
 Fer *me,* his Ole Black Mammy.

An' den de wartime hit bruck loose
 An' he up an' volumteered.
I couldn't sleep at night for years,
 Mah ole heart wuz jes' dat skeered,
An' ev'ry night on mah ole knees
 I'd pray fer Uncle Sammy,
An' dat *he'd* come *safe* back home **again**
 Ter me, his Ole Black Mammy.

An' when he come back frum de war,
　　He warn't a *boy* no longer;
His eyes looks sorter fur away,
　　An' his *jaw,* hit *sot* lots stronger.
But he grab hole to bofe mah hands,
　　Dem so ole an' black an' clammy,
An' sez, "God bless yo' precious soul,"
　　An' *hugged* his Ole Black Mammy!

I'se done de best I knows, deah Lawd,
　　But ef *he's* done air thing wrong,
When Jedgment comes I begs you to
　　Put de blame whar it belong,
'Cause I don't 'mount ter much *no* how;
　　Please 'scuse mah own pet Lam'my,
Jes' take him in an' shet *me* out—
　　Jes' *me,* his Ole Black Mammy.

MAH OLE MARSTER AN' MAH MISTIS

Dedicated to Mr. Jim Whitaker, Civil War Veteran,
Centreville, Miss.

You done ax me 'bout mah wartimes
   An' I done tole you all I knowed;
You done talked all 'bout mah 'ligion
   An' how awful *ole* I'se growed.
But when you ax me 'bout ole Marster
   An' mah Mistis—dis ole mouf
Could keep a-clackin' on till doomsday
   'Bout dey doin's in de Souf.

Mah ole Marster wuz a gent'man
   Frum his bootheels to his head;
You could tell dat he wuz "qual'ty"
   Frum de fust word dat he said.
He could do de softes' cussin'!
   Make yo' hair rise on yo' head,
An' de quickes' on de trigger!
   What he aimed at, Boss, wuz dead.

An' mah little bit o' Mistis—
   Lawsey Massey on mah soul,
I jes' b'lieve de Lawd He made her
   Out de pures' solid gole.
When she stood up side o' Marster
   He wuz taller by a head,
But she cu'd twis' him 'round her finger
   Lak you'd twis' a piece o' thread!

Once he sold a setter puppy
    Dat mah Mistis 'lowed ter keep—
Said he had enuf widout 'im
    An' cu'd sell him fer a heap.
Den nex' day he sed ter Mistis,
    "Splendid price I got fer Jack,"
An' she laf an' pat his arm an' tell 'im,
    "I doubled it ter git 'im back."

'Long in fall mah Marster tell me,
    "Pack mah grips, I'm goin' away—
Take a trip down ter de city,
    Guess I'll see de ponies play—
See mah frien's an' play some poker—
    Pick me up a little cash;
Feller's apt ter lose 'is ginger
    'Less he cuts a 'casional dash."

Den he'd come back bringin' Mistis
    Loads o' presents grand an' fine—
Maybe finger-rings or bres'pins,
    Or di'mun' earrings—how dey'd shine!
An' he'd kiss her han' an' tell her
    How he'd missed her, sho's you bawn,
But his bizness kep' 'im hus'lin
    Eve'y minute while he's gone.

An' Law, de doin's at de C'ris'mus!
  I cu'd talk a day er two,
Jes' ter 'scribe de drinks an' eatin's,
  An' de frolic'in' dey wu'd do.
Passin' silver mugs o' eggnog
  Ter de gues' wi'din de door;
Sendin' mons'tuous C'ris'mus baskets
  'Roun' de country ter de poor.

Table breakin' down wid goodies—
  Mandy's cookin' can't be beat;
Midnight dancin', an' mah Mistis
  Lak a feather on her feet;
An' mah Marster, bowin', scrapin'
  Ter de ladies ole an' young,
Passin' out dem pretty speeches
  Lak he had er silver tongue!

I done fix Marse Bob his toddy
  Eve'y mawnin' since he's grown.
I ain't drunk none since he lef' me—
  Seems ter choke me lak a bone.
I ain't good fer nothin', white folks;
  I'm de lonesomest nigger bawn
Since mah Marster an' mah Mistis
  All dis time am dead an' gone.

Parson talk to us 'bout Heaben,
  An' whut we'll fin' dere when we go;
I wants ter fin' mah Mistis smilin'
  An' er hummin' "Dixie" soft an' low.
I wants ter hear Marse Bob a-hollerin'
  Lak he allus useter 'fo' he died:
"You lazy, triflin', worthless rascal,
  I'm gwine skin you hair and hide."

When I'd git sick or full o' troubles
  Dere'd be Mistis, good an' kind,
An' mah Marster joshin' wid me,
  Jes' ter sorter 'stract mah mind.
Lawd, it's hard enuf ter live widout 'em—
  I gits mo' lonesomer dan sin.
But how's I gwinter *die* widout 'em?
  I jes' don't b'lieve dis nigger kin!

JIMMY JAY

I used to say I lak'd *all* birds
    Dat come up roun' de place;
I used to think dey all wuz sweet
    A-weavin' nests lak lace;
But one I didn't lak a'tall,
    Couldn' 'bide 'im fer a day,
An' I called 'im "Upstart-Smarty,"
    An' "Ole Squawkin' Jimmy Jay."

He use' ter plague me ter mah soul,
    A-streakin' roun' so fast,
Each squawkin' one a-zoonin' by
    I'd hope 'ud be de last.
Dey's a funny thing 'bout Jay birds,
    Folks tell me on de level,
You never sees 'em Fridays,
    Dey spen's *dem* wid de devil.

Tho' *I'm* a country bumpkin true,
    I sometime goes ter town,
An' when I does, I dresses up
    An' does de thing up brown.
Las' July Fo'th I ambles in
    An' wuz steppin' high an' gay,
Rat 'bove mah haid dat rascal squeal,
    "Jay—Jay—Coun-try Jay."

He sho' do rile me up sometime,
    Lak one day las' gone fall
I'se tryin' ter drive mah shoats t' town
    An' dey wouldn' go a'tall,
An' one dart in betwixt mah feet
    An' knock me silly—come—day,
An' dere he's squawkin' on de fence,
    "Goody fer you! Goody fer you!
        Jay—Jay!"

But you know somehow dat tricky bird
    He done turn't our hearts all to'rd him:
First time we took Josephus out
    Dat bird ack lak he know'd him;
Dat bird an' pickaninny
    Dey both sets out to play,
Each one a-tryin' ter bust his lungs
    A-hollerin' "Jay—Jay—Jay."

Seem lak he laugh ez plain to me
    Ez any folks I ever heard.
He steals de fruit an' meddles 'round,
    De *peskiest,* loudes' bird;
But he seem ter 'muse Josephus so,
    Make 'im laugh an' clap an' play,
Till we's sorter got a 'tachment now
    Fer dat noisy Jimmy Jay.

An' once when Mandy lay so low
    All de doctors wuz in doubt,
An' I had ter dose her reg'lar
    Or she sho'ly would pass out,
I was dat beat out an' fell asleep—
    An' I'd be a lonesom' soul today
Ef he hadn't passed de winder
    Jus' a-squallin' "Jay—Jay."

So he's sorter lak Josephus now,
    Wid his hid'jeus ole tin horn
A-raisin' bigger ructions
    Eve'y day since he been born—
But we couldn't spare Josephus
    Not a single, solid day,
An' we'se sorter got ter feelin'
    Jes' de same 'bout Jimmy Jay.

RASTUS' FIRST BALL GAME

All mah life, ez I kin well recall,
I'se heerd of a game dey call "Baseball;"
An' tho' I'se often heerd de name,
I never yit had seed a game;
So when I larnt de yuther day
De Mobile Bears wuz a-gwinter play
De Memphis Chicks at old Russwood,
I vow'd I'd be dere ef I could.

So dere I wuz, when de game wuz call'—
Dem Chic'saw Injuns ain't Injuns a'tall!
I shore wuz good an' 'sprized all right
Ter find dey ev'y one wuz white;
An' de Mobile Bears, fer all dey noise,
Ain' nothin' but common long 'Merican boys,
An' I'd lak to ax somebody whut knows
Whar'd dey *git* dem outdachious clothes.

When I sets down a feller came
An' sets by me fer ter view de game,
An' he sho'ly wuz a scrapper *right*—
He done all he could fer ter make 'em *fight;*
"Hit 'im Kid! Knock 'im dead!
Bust 'im in de nose!" an' sich, he said;
"Come on here, you crazy Jake,
Give us a hit fer Heaven's sake!"

A man he wuz tryin' ter pitch a ball
Ter hit a stick, but *couldn't* a'tall,
An' a funny man in a blue serge suit
Ack lak a nat'chel born crazy galoot;
He'd shake his fist an' rave an' shout
Till I thought de cops'd put him *out;*
"Strike!" he'd yell, an' "Strike!" he'd *squall,*
But de feller jes' kep' on *pitchin'* de ball.

An' de feller dat wuz dere a settin' by me
Sez: "I wonder how many fans we see?"
An' *I* sez, "Man, you is shore one *dunce,*
'Cause I ain't seed nobody *fannin'* once."
Den he sez, "Hey!—Dixie stole a base,"
But ev'y *bag* wuz still in place;
An' den he sez, "Dere goes a *fly,*
But it ain't no good—it went too high."

An' dere wuzn't a single fly in *sight*
Altho' I looked wid all mah might;
An' 'bout dat time, de ball *hit* de stick
An' bounce *way* off, real fas' an' *quick.*
De man wid de stick ain't got no sense
Bounce a *fine* ball plum' over de fence,
Gran' stan' folks *clap* an' ack *glad*
So de po' boy won't feel so *bad.*

An' one ole feller mus'-a been in disgrace—
Had a kind o' frame work hidin' his face—
An' in all dis happy land o' love
I never seed sech a mons'tuous glove.
An' when it's all over and time ter go
De Bears had nuthin' and de Chicks had fo',
An' it look'd ter me lak de foolishest game
But I sho' do lak it jus' de same.

COMIN' HOME AGAIN

I'se been away frum mah ole home
   An' done stayed fer quite a while,
An' you don' know de lonesomeness
   Dat I'se been thru' wi'd, chile.
I stayed away a mons'tuous time
   'Cause I wuz boun' and had to do it,
But it took all de sand I had
   Fer ter pull dis nigger thru' it.
You find good folks most ev'ywhere
   An' deys friendly in de main,
But dey couldn't wean mah heart away
   Frum comin' home again.

I'd do ve'y well endurin' de day
   'Cause I'd be busy bustlin' round,
But mah heart it went to sinkin'
   When de sun kep drappin' down,
An' de hoot owls in de bushes
   Made mah flesh turn col' and creep,
An' I know'd I'd tramp a hund'ed miles
   Fer ter git in home ter sleep
Or set inside my cabin do',
   An' watch de fallin' rain
An' thank de Lawd an' Marster
   Fer bein' home again.

I'd wander roun' so res'less
    Dat I'd almos' lose mah mind;
It didn't he'p a single bit
    Ef folks *wuz* good an' kind.
I couldn' rest or sleep o' nights
    Or find no taste fer food.
When folks 'ud pass de time o' day
    I couldn' match dey mood,
'Cause nuthin' you can beg nor buy
    Can ease dat ache an' pain—
Can't nuthin' cease dat misery
    But comin' home again.

Durin' dis pas' gone war time
    Dey call "homesick" a disease;
Ef you ain't never had it
    Jus' be thankful on yo' knees.
Dey say dat some dem soldiers,
    In spite o' grit an' pride,
Jes' miss dey home and folks *so* bad
    Dey jes' give up an' died.
But I know Good Ole Saint Peter
    Welcome *dem* wid might an' main
'Cause dat's de onliest chance *dey* had
    O' comin' home again.

An' I guess it's jus' intended
    As a lesson we mus' find
To mek us 'preciate home de mo'
    An' be mo' good an' kind,
'Cause folks whut goes so fer away
    An' stays dere satisfied,
Ain't meant *much to* dey home, I guess,
    An' dey ain't nobudy's pride.
Fer ef you ain't felt homesickness—
    Dat awful gnawin' pain—
Den you can't know de blessed feel
    O' comin' home again.

I'se done ben ter stracted meetin'
    Ob de bigges' and de best,
I'se done tended big baptizens,
    An' outshouted *all* de rest,
I'se done marched wid Sons o' Zion,
    An' done seen big league baseball,
An' still mah bones ain't satisfied
    Wid none dem things a'tall;
'Cause I'm standin' here ter tell you
    Dat all dem joys is vain;
Dey can't *tech* de bustin' glory
    O' comin' home again.

SAMBO IN CHICAGO

De days am dark an' sad an' dreary,
  Dis Northland sho' am bleak and cold;
Mah heart feels lonesome-like an' weary—
  Lak a lamb what's lost from out de fold.
Ef I was just back down in Dixie,
  In de land o' cotton where I used to be,
Just once mo' back in Memphis,
  Good ole Memphis, Tennessee.

White folks, I wuz bawn in Memphis,
  An' done live dere all mah life,
Dat's whar I bu'ied my mammy, and
  Dat's whar I mah'ied my wife.
I got friends dere by de dozen,
  White and black, to stan' by me;
Ef I could make it back to Memphis,
  Good ole Memphis, Tennessee.

I heerd dem Yankee strangers talkin'
  'Bout de wages I could git
Ef I'd go up North long wid 'em,
  So like a fish I up an' bit.
An' altho' dey treats me han'some
  An' is kind as dey can be,
All I studies 'bout is Memphis,
  Good ole Memphis, Tennessee.

I wish dem niggers down on Beale Street
    Could just ha'f know de fix I'm in,
Dey'd just git up one mo' crap game
    An' up an' sen' me what dey win;
Enough to buy a one-way ticket,
    Dat's just all 'twould take fer me
Just ter git me back to Memphis,
    Good ole Memphis, Tennessee.

I can hear dem niggers strummin'
    On de banjo soft an' low,
An' a-comin' down de ribber
    I can hear Kate Adams blow.
She's due now at de landin'
    An' I'm blue as I can be—
'Cause I, too, am due in Memphis,
    Good ole Memphis, Tennessee.

When I goes to church on Sundays,
    An' hear de preachin' an' de songs,
I ax de Lord fer jes' one thing—
    To git me back whar I belongs.
An' when Gabriel toots his trumpet,
    An' de las' day dawns fer me,
Jes' ter let me die in Memphis,
    Good ole Memphis, Tennessee.

An' when I gits to Heaben,
   An' we're passin' down de line
To view dem glory mansions,
   All made of stuffs dat shine,
I'm gwinter tell mah Marster
   Dat ef dey ain't no place fer me
He can send me back to Memphis,
   Good ole Memphis, Tennessee.

OUR MOCKIN' BIRD

I want ter ax yo'all white folks
   Fer ter gimme all yo'alls' word
Dat you won't let yo' play chillun
   Kill air' single mockin' bird.
Ef dey ain't never heerd one
   Wake in de night an' sing,
Dey don't know, ter kill one
   Is ter do a mons'tuous thing.

Dere's one whut's been a comin'
   Ter de same big ole oak tree
Fer de three las' pas' gone summers
   An' he seems lak folks ter me.
An' of'en in de ebenin',
   When I'm mendin' on mah boat,
Dat sassy rascal whistles
   Lak he's tryin' ter bust his throat.

I spec yo'all knows mah Mandy—
   She can wash de pretties' clo'se
An' spile mo' white folks chillun
   De Lawd o' Massey knows.
But she's gittin' ole an' feeblesome
   Since our boy, he went ter war,
An' got kilt up by dem furriners,
   Way off f'um home so far.

When we hears dat mocker warblin'
It peartens us a heap,
An' one time jus' fo' mornin'
I heerd a "peep, peep, peep."
"Somepin' got yo' chickens, Mandy,
You better rise up out dat bed!"
"Dat's dat mockin' bird, Erastus;
What's de matter wid yo' head?"

Now, our boy we named Josephus,
Fer de Bible book, you know;
But his Cap'n says de soldiers
Allus called him "Whis'lin' Joe."
'Cause no diff'rince whut de matter wuz
In all dat reg-i-ment,
He says dat boy wuz whis'lin'
No matter whar he went.

An' dat mornin' when de message come
Fer ter tell us Joe wuz dead,
I heerd dat mocker whis'lin'
Fo' I got up out o' bed.
An' I sed "Jes' lissen, Mandy,
At dat bird a whis'lin' so—
It soun' jes' lak Josephus,
Right dar, comin' in de do'!"

'Cose, you know, we never 'grudged him
    Fer ter he'p his Uncle Sammy,
But he's de onliest chick or chile we had,
    An' it might nigh kilt his mammy.
She don't take no comfort much
    In nothin' she can see,
But only jes' dat mockin' bird
    A trillin' in de tree.

An' we sorter lowed between us
    In our lonesome little shack,
De Lawd don' sent dat mocker,
    Since Josephus can't come back,
Ter sorter cheer, and tell us
    Ef we does de best we know,
Dat when we gits ter Heaben
    We'll find our Whis'lin' Joe.

So won't yo'all ax de chillun
    To be careful ef dey please,
Not ter never, ever harm de birds
    Whut's trillin' in de trees.
'Cause dis world am full o' troubles,
    Sich as dey ain't never heerd,
An' our hearts jes' needs de comfort
    Of de Blessed Mockin' Bird.

RASTUS IN DISTRESS

Far from home de news done reach' me
    De ole Miss'sip' am on a tear,
Done rose up an' oberflowin'
    Bustin' lebbys ev'ywhere.
Lawd, what de matter wid dat ribber,
    It done had to cut de buck?
Ain't de folks down in mah Soufland
    Had enuf o' rotten luck?

I done seed her once rampagin'
    An' I can't fergit de sight,
People runnin', cryin', prayin',
    In de dead 'ours uv de night.
Tain't no power on earth can hol' it
    When it once com'ence ter swell,
Ev'rything go' down befo' it,
    Jus' a ragin' rushin' hell.

I sho' is bothered 'bout mah white folks,
    All dey land is layin' low,
An' dat ole Miss'sip'll git 'em
    Jus' as sho's she oberflow.
Doan't know what's become o' mammy,
    May be daid for all I know,
She wuz livin' wid mah white folks
    Jus' out 'hine dey kitchen do'.

Who gwine save mah boss's b'longin's?
(Jus' one man dere wid his wife),
Who gwine save his fine, fat cattle?
Dey do well ter save dey life.
Where dey goin' ter go for 'tection?
Neighbors in de selfsame boat,
Lawdy; when I studies 'bout it
Some'pin gits me by de th'oat.

Can't no human stop dat 'struction,
It's beyond de power o' man;
Lawd, step in an' he'p mah people—
You's de onliest one what can—
An' let me fin' 'em when I gits dere
Somewhar, Marster, safe an' soun',
When dat mons'tuous ragin' ribber
Mak her min' up to go down.

DE TRY-STATE FARE

I be'n ter Memphis, ter de Try-State Fare,
An' de whole of Kingdom Come wuz dere.
De Lawsy Massey upon mah soul!
I didn' know dis worl' could hol'
Ez many folks ez I would meet
Back'uds and for'uds on de street.

I be'n a savin' so dis fall
I could see dat Fare and a game o' ball.
'Course I went to'ds de Fare Groun' firs',
Wid mah baseball money tuck 'way in mah purse;
An' Honey, lemme tell you 'twuz a mortal sin,
De money dat man at de gate took in!

Well, I went in an' I roamed aroun'—
Dere couldn't a' be'n a soul uptown.
Folks wuz a-swarmin' thick ez bees—
Eben on de outside, up in trees.
A body'd a' thought dat de Jedgment trump
Had de whole o' creation on de jump.

Betcher eve'l las' soul from ole Miss'sip
Had done lef' home fer ter take dis trip,
An' de whole blame State of Arkansaw
Had jus' splurged in wid a big hur-raw.
'Twould take all de rest o' mah life ter tell
Of de things dey had ter see an' sell.

In all mah days sence I be'n born,
I never seed sich ears o' corn—
Fruits an' stuff so fine an' nice,
Must'er be'n growed in Pair'o'dice;
Hawses an' cattle, so fat an' fine—
I wish jes' one o' dem hawgs wuz mine!

I went all 'roun' frum place ter place,
An' viewed de 'zibits an' seed 'um race—
Folks runnin' autos lak de's mad;
En I sez ter mah se'f, "Ef it ain't too bad,
Memphis an' Fote Wurth playin' ball,
Ain't got nobody ter see 'um at all."

I jes' decided dey wouldn' play—
Jes' put it off 'till ernother day.
So I jes' kep' lookin' an' hanging roun'.
But, bless mah soul! on de way up town,
We passed Russwood fo' early dark,
An' a billion folks wuz leavin' dat park.

An' when I got off at ole Main Street,
De folks up town wuz a sight ter beat.
You shore cu'd a sold me fer a dime;
Dere I be'n a-thinkin' all de time
Dat all de folks dat de worl' cu'd spare
Wuz out dere takin' in de Try-State Fare.

Dat ole Memphis is sho' some town,
But she gotta compass in a heap mo' groun'
Else she'll fin' in a yeah or two,
Folks jes' a-flockin' dere lak dey do,
Be no place ter draw yo' bref—
Youall Memphis folks, better hump yo'sef.

"MAH OLE DOG"

I knows I'se poor an' 'umble
　　An' had troubles all mah days,
I knows mah state is lowly
　　An' don't many sing mah praise.
I knows mah life is lonely
　　Lak I'se los' out in de fog,
But I'se got som'pin *some* ain't got—
　　De fines' ole houn' dog!

He dozes dere 'long 'side mah chair
　　Ez long ez I'm a settin',
An' follers ra't dere at mah heels
　　When de chores and wood I'se gettin'.
Ef I ambles off to'ds town sometime
　　Fer a little peaceful jog,
Mah bes' frien' always 'companys me,
　　Dis same ole good houn' dog.

Once we wuz awful po'ly
　　An' Mammy had er spell,
We didn' have no rations
　　Ner nothin' we could sell,
A man whut coon hunts tol' me
　　Dat he'd swap a fine fat hog
Fer us ter kill an' eat on
　　Ef I'd let 'im have mah dog.

An' when I axes Mammy
    Whut she think erbout dat deal,
She sez "We's got some 'lasses
    An' a little mo' cawn meal;
An' is you done fergit de night
    Lost in dat frozen bog,
You didn't know *which* way *wuz* home
    But he did, dat ole houn' dog?"

An' so we'se kep' 'im wid us,
    Tho' little else we'se had,
But endurin' our privations
    We hasn't felt so bad,
In fac', sometimes you sees me
    All puffed up lak a frog
At some de smart gyrations
    Of dat same ole fine houn' dog.

Dere ain't so many folkses
    Dat'll stand yo' frien' fer life,
Dey's mighty apt ter turn you down
    When troubles come, an' strife,
But I'se got one ter stick by me
    Till he's dead ez any log,
You might say "He ain't human,"
    But he *is*—mah ole houn' dog!

"HA'NTS"

Chillun, I jes wants ter ax you
  Is you ever seed a ha'nt?
Is you had dat awful 'sperience
  Dat you wants ter run an' can't?
Is you felt yo' flesh a-creepin'
  An' yo' hair rise on yo' head
When you hears day bones a-rattlin',
  An' you sees de walkin' dead?

'Bout a week ago come Sunday,
  In de stilles' dead of night
I woke from deepes' slumberin'
  Jus' 'bout froze stiff wid fright.
I could hear sich awful moanin'
  An' sich groanin' ra't close by
Dat I know'd fer shore som'body
  Wuz a gwine ter up an' die.

I jes' bus' mah door wide open
  Wid de hardes', swiftes' kick.
In de nex' room wuz mah Mammy
  An' she wuz so *pow'rful* sick
Dat I know'd I couldn't he'p her
  An' dat hour would be her last
Ef I didn' fetch de Doctor—
  An' I better fetch him fast.

Now twixt us ole place an' Doctor's,
   ('Cause he's livin' up nigh town,)
Is a place we all fights shy of,
   We calls it de buryin' groun',
An' you can bet yo' bottom dollar
   Since Marse Noah built de ark
Ain't a nigger in dese regions
   Dat's done passed dere after dark.

But I seed I had ter do it,
   An' I couldn't wait till day,
So I co't my mule an' started
   (I wuz prayin' all de way—)
When I loped up 'side de graveyard
   Lawd, mah heart wuz in mah feet,
An' ra't dere by de roadside
   Wuz a sight dat can't be beat.

It wuz tall an' white an' shiny,
   An' it shook lak it wuz cold;
White beard all down its buzzom
   Lak dem Prophet Kings of old;
Its arms wuz long an' skinny
   An' its feet don't tech de groun';
It come oozin' from dat graveyard
   An' it didn't make a soun'.

An' it whinkered lak a squeech owl
   An' wuz travelin' lak de win',
It wuz headed ra't straight at me
   An' I yelled an' kicked lak sin,
Fer mah teeth wuz jes' a-clickin'
   An' mah blood hit done run cold
When I feel its hot breath on me
   An' its hands jes' grabbin' hold.

Den dat good fer nothin' jug-head
   Took *dat* time ter up an' balk,
I ain't stop ter argue wid 'im,
   I ain't got no time fer talk.
I jes' split dat road wide open
   Wid mah head an' wid mah heels,
An' I seed dem ha'nts jes' ev'ywhere,
   Long de road an' in de fiels.

Chile, I bus' in on dat Doctor,
   An' mos' skeer dat man ter death,
Den he says, "Hitch up de buggy,
   I'll go wid yer; ketch yo' *breath.*"
An' when we drove back *by dere*
   (Doctors allus is so brave),
Every ha'nt dat I'd been 'scribin
   Done crawl' ra't back down in dey grave.

"MAH MAMMY"

Of late yeahs in de Springtime
　　Dere's a day whut's set apart
For "Mothers' Day" dey call it,
　　An' it might nigh breaks mah heart
'Cause dem whut's got dey Mammy
　　Wears a red rose on dey breast,
But *me,* I wears a white one,
　　'Cause mah Mammy's laid ter rest.

I never know'd whut trouble wuz
　　Ez long ez she could share it,
I never lacked fer nothin' yet
　　Ef she had it an' *could spare* it.
She taught me all on earth I knows
　　An' she loved me an' she praised me,
I guess I wouldn't 'mount ter much
　　Ef dat Mammy hadn't raised me.

She taught me 'bout de country's laws,
　　An' how I must obey 'em,
She read me 'bout de Lawd an' prayers,
　　An' taught me how ter say 'em;
Ter pay mah debts an' mind mah job,
　　An' not ter swear nor fuss,
An' I guess widout mah Mammy
　　I'd a been a wuthless cuss.

When I wuz jes' a little tad
　An' times wuz close an' tight,
She'd hire out ter de white folks
　An' work frum morn till night.
She'd wash dey clothes an' curtains
　An' soap, an' souse, an' rub,
Seem lak mah Mammy's back 'ud break
　A-bendin' 'cross dat tub.

An' den she'd cook dey vittles
　Jus' de best dat she wuz able,
An' dish it up an' set it out
　An' call dem ter de table.
So what wuz left dey gave ter her
　An' she'd fetch it home ter me,
When I'd done et all I could hold
　She'd eat whut's left, you see.

Den she'd set dere in de do' way
　An' take me on her knee
An' talk an' sing an' rock me
　Jes' as happy as could be,
An' ax me whut I'se done all day,
　Ef I'se been happy an' content;
She always took big int'res' like
　Till de very day she went.

An' when I grow'd up older den,
    An' cu'd hire out too an' work,
I found de world wuz hard enough,
    But I wouldn't laze ner shirk,
'Cause mah Mammy wuz a hustler
    An' she sho' cu'd mak me shame,
Er sayin' ef *I'se* triflin' dat
    I'd lose *her* her good name.

An' ef I'd use po' jedgment
    Dat would git me in a tight,
I foun' folks turnin' frum me
    Sayin' "You ain't acted right."
But I foun' out one thing certain,
    An' it didn' take me long,
Dat mah Mammy *she* wuz fer me,
    Ef I'se either *right* or *wrong*.

An' when we laid her in de grave
    I know'd my sun wuz set,
Mah heart jes' started breakin'
    An' it's achin' fer her yet.
Dis world hit seem a doleful place
    An' de days too long at dat,
An' my notion Lawd uv Heaben
    Ez whar mah Mammy's at.

TO A LITTLE GIRL

Hair of gold—like sunshine falling;
　　Eyes? Well, grey, I guess—but, too,
They are deep and clear as Heaven
　　And can look me thro' and thro'.
Feet that flit about so swiftly
　　Tipping up to see the world,
Lips that frame so many questions,
　　That's my own, My Little Girl.

Songs that she's heard someone singing
   She will trill and sing to me,
But in a moment tears are falling,
   Oh! perhaps she's bumped her knee;
But Mother's kisses heal it quickly,
   Back again to play she'll whirl,
And once more she's singing, smiling,
   Such a happy little girl.

Then to kindergarten trudging
   As our girlies must, you know,
Mother, watching at the window,
   Loves, yet dreads, to see her go.
Going forth to leave her mother,
   One step further in the world.
Oh! that she were always only
   Just a little, little girl.

Oh! the many plans that circle
   'Round that bobbing golden head,
And the long, long thoughts outstretching
   To her future, far ahead.
Hopes and prayers oft intermingled,
   That of *this,* my precious pearl,
Fate will be so *very* careful
   Of my own, my little girl.

SERVICE

To N. W.

I know a heart that is so kind—
Guile in no man can he find;
A heart so free from self, indeed,
He never sees what he might need,
But always quick and eager to
Devote his time to me and you.

He scarce can wait the seeming hour
To do all things within his power
To smooth the path and ease the way,
To something kind and soothing say,
To just forestall the every need—
Oh, but he is a friend indeed.

So many things his heart can hold—
My cares, and yours, oh, hundredfold!
And when my calm is sadly shaken
And to him my woes I've taken,
He simply smooths all wrinkles out,
Vanish all my fear and doubt!

There are those who *promise* well,
But are forgetting while we tell,
But tho' perhaps he's far away
And bigger deeds may fill his day,
I find the thing I'd pondered o'er
Has been done for me—and more.

Such seeing eyes I've never known,
Such kindly thoughts were never shown,
Such quickening steps to welcome one,
Such joy he shows in what you've done,
Such service to us all he gives,
God bless him every day he lives!

ME AND M' MOTHER

'Course, I ain't so very old, I know;
    I'm jus' four years old today,
An' I spec' that you'll be thinkin'
    I better run on out an' play.
Jes' 'cause I've never been to school,
    Nor rode street cars alone,
You needn't think I never had
    A n'idear of my own.
Tho' I don't lissun to the grown-folks
    When they talk to one another,
Still I knows jus' lots o' things—
    Jus' things—'bout—Me and m' Mother.

I'll bet you she's the bestes' one
    That ever yet was born,
An' she gave me fer m' birthday
    The biggest stripedy horn;
An' when I blow right hard on it
    It makes the biggest noise—
I never heard one like it—
    Of any girl's or boy's.
An' I let m' Sister blow it some,
    An' two or free times m' Brother;
But I was only lendin' them—
    It b'longs to Me an' m' Mother.

An' once when I had m' wagon
In the back yard haulin' wood,
That big ole turkey gobbler
Chased me jus' as fas' he could;
An' all the other children
What was in our yard to play,
They laughed and poked their tongues at me
An' said, "Shamey," "Shamey"—jus' that way.
So I jus' left 'em playin'
Out there with one another,
An' I went in our kitchen
An' played—jus' Me an' m' Mother.

An' nen I climbed the banister rail
An' slipped off on the stair,
An' fell forty-levun stairsteps,
Nen bumped into a chair.
I thought my skull was fractioned
An' my right arm broken, too;
So I laid still an' held m' breath—
'Twas all that I could do.
Nen she runned from out her room,
Where she's sewing for m' Brother,
An' grabbed me up an' kissed me,
An' we cried then—Me an' m' Mother.

'Course, you know I love my Daddy—
　　He's as fine as any one;
He gives me jits and tumbles me,
　　An' is jus' the mostes' fun;
An' I like most all my kinfolks,
　　So when they come and go
I do feel sorter lonesome-like
　　An' things are sorter slow.
Nen, when they has to go school,
　　I miss my Sister and m' Brother,
But still—I'm jus' as satyfied
　　To play—jus' Me and m' Mother.

Well, after I have played all day
　　An' come crawlin' in her lap,
She hugs me up an' says to me:
　　"You are sleepy, little chap;
Come on and put your nightie on
　　Just as fast as fast can be,
Because I can hear the Sandman,
　　And he's after you and me."
She tucks me in, and Daddy comes
　　Fer one kiss, nen another;
Nen she kneels down 'side my bed
　　An' we pray—jus' Me an' m' Mother.

TRUTHFUL(?) GEORGE

In the month of February
Comes Valentine so bright and cheery,
Then the birthday of the fellow
Who was never 'fraid nor yellow.
"Our George," we say with pride,
"The only boy who never lied."

Do you grown folks all believe it,
Can your minds for *true* conceive it,
That a man who was so great,
To be our President was his fate,
Could have held out till he died
And not a single time have lied?

I know some boys 'at's pretty good—
Bring in kindlin', chop the wood;
But they *do* deceive the wimmin'.
Have to *lie* to go in swimmin';
I know George's *Pa* has sighed
'Bout his boy who never lied.

Wonder was he *very* good
Or if *his Pa* just—understood?
George would never do no kickin',
Just stood up and took his lickin'.
He must'a had some grit and pride,
Or else he *shorely* would've lied.

Is it as the hist'ries tell,
Or did he *lie,* but do it *well?*
I'd like to be as good as he,
But you'd better not depend on me,
'Cause when I'm *skeered,* I'm 'fraid I've lied,
I did it tho' to save my *hide.*

THE COUNTRY DOCTOR

Dedicated to Dr. Wm. L. Goddard, Saulsbury, Tenn.

The histories tell of Heroes
　Who fought amidst the fray,
And tell of their brave martyrs
　Who lived in bygone day.
But in the Hall of Fame it seems
　This picture should be hung—
"The Old Time Country Doctor,
　Unhonored and Unsung."

He first greets us in this world
　And as gently sends us out;
Our Doctor, true, he is, we know,
　But a Friend without a doubt.
He travels long and weary miles
　To ease us in our pain,
And while we sleep he turns about
　And travels on again.

He has but few devices there
　To assist him in his task,
Nor the help of good trained nurses—
　Some neighbor he must ask.
No fine swift car does he possess
　To rush from call to call,
But drives a sleek old honest horse
　Who seldom sees his stall.

Sometimes his collar's wrinkled,
  Ofttimes he needs a shave,
But he's no time to give himself—
  There's someone's life to save.
For he must make the weary trip
  As fast as he is able,
Much-needed food he leaves untouched
  Upon the waiting table.

He does not heal the flesh alone,
  But advises, comforts, sorrows,
O'er his patients' troubled yesterdays
  And the problems of their 'morrows.
There's not one hour of day or night
  That he claims for his own—
A martyr to his countryside
  If one was ever known.

But when his patients rally
  And are eased from pain and fright,
They oft forget the frantic call
  They sent in dead of night.
They have rich food and raiment fine
  And travel all about,
While one who gave the best he had
  Must somehow do without.

We note how very tired he looks,
    How thin and worn he seems,
He's served us well in rain or shine
    And few have been his dreams;
And when he's given all his strength
    And can minister no more,
Our tear-filled eyes behold one day
    A wreath on "Doctor's" door.

We know he's found a place at last
    Where he can sleep and rest.
No midnight call awakes him
    Nor a care his days infest.
And I think up there in God's House
    There's a silence sweet and deep,
That the Angels all tread softly
    Because "Doctor" is asleep.

MY MIND AND YOURS

My mind is like a butterfly,
  Or a swift-winged humming bird:
It stops not any place for long
  Nor makes its singing heard.
O'er perfumed flowers it drifts and sails
  And tastes not very deep;
But tho' it darts so lightly 'round,
  It never knoweth sleep.

Your mind is big and broad and fine
  And moves on stately wings;
It does not seek the flowers alone
  And leave the worthier things.
I know that you great wisdom glean,
  And I go not so deep,
But I am ever wide awake
  And love you while you sleep.

And *there* we have a common ground
  Where both minds meet as one,
For *my* knowledge, dear, of loving
  Is the deepest 'neath the sun.
And when you hold me 'gainst your heart
  In this golden evening weather,
What cares *your* wondrous mind or *mine*
  If we're scribes or fools together?

"AND THERE'S THAT!"

A girl there was—
　And her wit was rare;
Her form was perfect,
　Her face was fair.
Her ways were charming
　And full of grace,
And—she fell in love
　With a handsome *face*.

She left her home
　And her mother's side,
To go with him
　As a happy Bride,
And found that instead
　Of love and thrills—
A handsome face
　Can't pay the bills.

RIDING ON THE TRAIN

There are many things
   In this world of woe
That may please us, or vex us,
   As we onward go;
That may give us a thrill
   Or give us a pain,
Or *bore* us to death—
   Such as—riding a train.

You stroll on the monster
   Just as fresh as a queen,
And in less than ten minutes
   You're not fit to be seen.
You're shiny and hot,
   All your primping is vain,
You *look* like a wreck—
   When riding the train.

When everyone's on and
   The coaches are full,
We're off with a toot
   And a jerk and a pull.
Tho' grinding and screeching
   May cause your soul pain,
Just grin and endure it—
   You're riding the train!

You try to be calm, and
  Sit stately and still,
And are nearly knocked senseless
  Descending a hill;
You try to converse some,
  But all that is vain,
You must just sit there speechless,
  And *ride* on the train!

You get out a novel
  And think you will read,
You find to your sorrow
  You are mistaken, indeed;
For four boys behind you
  With might and with main
Are doing their darndest
  To tear up the train.

And would you seek slumber,
  You poor, weary dear,
Then 'long comes the butcher
  And yells in your ear.
You long for a bludgeon
  That butcher to brain,
But think of him kindly,
  He lives on the train.

Here comes the conductor,
  Collecting your fare;
You hand him your ticket
  And give him a *glare*.
And a red-hot fury
  Is racking your brain,
For you're paying *good* money
  To ride on the train.

When eternities pass and
  Your journey ends,
And you collapse in the arms
  Of your waiting friends,
You say, "Oh, thank Heaven,"
  And, "Never again,"
Or—"I'll be riding feet foremost
  When I next ride a train."

But still—when you're bored
  With just sitting at home,
With a weary spirit
  That longs to roam—
Now, how can you do it?
  Just answer me plain.
Why, pack up your suitcase
  And *ride on the train!*

"MEMPHIS DOWN IN DIXIE"

Song—(Air, "Where the River Shannon Flows")

There's a land across the ocean
That has my heart's devotion,
And though in this foreign country
There are cities fine and grand,
Every moment I am yearning
Oh, I would be returning
To the dear old town of Memphis
In the heart of Dixie Land.

CHORUS

Oh, Memphis, down in Dixie,
You are the Southland's pride,
And for you your boys in khaki
Have so bravely fought and died.
There a joyous welcome waits me
For they're a loyal band,
In the dear old town of Memphis
In the heart of Dixie Land.

There I left my dear old mother
And the girl I love behind me,
When my Uncle Sammy called me
To go and fight across the sea.
Now across these foreign borders
I am waiting for my orders
That will take me back to Memphis
In the heart of Dixie Land.

When my captain, brave and witty,
Casts his anchor in that city,
Where Miss Liberty is standing
With her torchlight in her hand,
I'll not pause to view her towers,
But spend life's golden hours
In the dear old town of Memphis
In the heart of Dixie Land.

TO KIT

On Thanksgiving Day

As I stroll with throngs this morning
    Churchward bound—Thanksgiving Day—
I hear them as they count their joys
    And I smile at what they say:
So thankful for possessions,
    They have hoarded, bit by bit;
But I sorrow for them secretly
    That they have not you, my Kit.

They are smug and most complacent
    O'er their balance at the bank,
For well-filled barns and groaning board
    The Lord they gravely thank.
And when they've filled the inner man,
    Then dully there they'll sit;
I pity them that they can't know
    The joy and life of Kit.

Most women of the normal type
    Adore their own complexion,
And thank the Lord most ardently
    If their features are perfection.
But what care I for sun or rain,
    Or if I rough or tan a bit,
If I know that I am blessed enough
    To be loved by you, my Kit?

A flash of sunlight thru' the rain,
    A smiling moon at night,
The rainbow when the tempest's past,
    A steady, burning light;
All things that comfort, warm and cheer,
    All of life that's good and fit:
These things and even more to me
    Have you always been, my Kit.

And when on each Thanksgiving Day
    My heart goes up to God,
To thank Him and to bless Him
    For His aid, as on I've trod,
I thank Him for the star you are
    And that my path you've lit—
I thank Him every year anew
    For giving me my Kit.

YOUR DEAR HAND

I wonder how I'd fared, dear,
　　If I had walked alone,
If loneliness and solitude
　　Had marked me for their own,
If I had made life's journey
　　Through a barren, loveless land,
If I'd not had your love, dear,
　　And had not held your hand.

Sometimes when life was dreary
　　And it seemed I could not see
Just why such heavy storm-clouds
　　Should blot the sun from me,
I'd feel my life-house rocking
　　On the shifting, slipping sand—
Oh! then I'd flee to you, love,
　　And cling to your dear hand.

And never would you question,
　　'Mid the cares and daily fret,
If I had grappled wisely
　　With the problems I had met.
But, oh, the joy to my tired heart
　　To know you'd understand,
To just look deep into your eyes
　　And hold your dear, warm hand.

And I think sometimes, you know, dear,
    That alone, I falter sadly,
For you give me so much of you
    And offer it so gladly.
And I think that I'm most blessed
    In all this wondrous land
Because you have journeyed with me
    And I have held your hand.

THE BLUEBIRD

I'm listening for you, Bluebird—
    It may be too early, though—
You know far more than I do
    About the ice and sleet and snow.
But the feel of Spring is absent
    And the Winter seems o'er long,
As I listen every morning
    For your happy Bluebird song.

The Robins and the Jaybirds
    Are so busy all around;
That adored and blessed Mocker
    Fills my garden with sweet sound.
But Nature's color scheme's unfinished
    And her symphony incomplete,
So spread those wings of Heaven's blueness
    And hasten to us, Bluebird, sweet.

It seems to me each Springtime
    That your Easter gown is bluer,
And that each gay, happy lovenote
    Is a little sweeter, truer.
You flutter past my casement
    Like a flake of Heaven-blue sky,
And my heart on wings goes with you
    As you fly, and fly, and fly.

And I wish my earthly spirit
  Could be transformed to a bird,
And I could sail on o'er the treetops
  And sing the sweetest ever heard.
And perhaps I'd meet you, Bluebird,
  And before we had to part
You'd whisper me the secret
  Of your happy, happy heart.

For the Bluebird is for Happiness—
  That's what the poet sings—
And our hearts are always gladdened
  By that flash of Heaven-blue wings.
And I think these loved joy bringers
  Must surely *never die,*
But they all have drifted upward
  And made the blue that's in the sky.

THE HAPPINESS HOUSE

There's a rambling, low-roofed cottage,
  Where the woods are cool and still,
On a shaded, dreamy, slope-side
  Where the road winds to the hill;
And the trees and birds and flowers
  Seem to know some fairy code,
In this little House o' Happiness
  That's built beside the road.

I have spent long years in questing
  After visions, rainbow-hued;
I have wasted soul and substance
  While these phantoms I pursued;
My heart could find no anchorage
  'Til I took up my abode
In this little House o' Happiness
  That's built beside the road.

My days were frantic strugglings,
  My nights were dream-wrecked waste;
My feet were ever stumbling
  In the mad on-rushing haste;
But Fate drew me to this threshold
  Where I cast aside my load
In this little House o' Happiness
  That's built beside the road.

Where the lacy, flickering shadows,
   Ever dancing on the wall,
But accentuate the silence
   And the peace that broods o'er all;
Where the stars and moonlight falling,
   Nowhere else so bright have glowed,
As on the little House o' Happiness
   That's built beside the road.

So, here in restful silences
   I watch the crowds stream by,
They are struggling toward the hilltop,
   There to grasp success or die;
And one, with many followers,
   Was cursing as he strode
Past the little House o' Happiness
   That's built beside the road.

They are crowding; greedy, envious,
   Each one seeking to be first;
No time for rest or pleasuring—
   For gain they are athirst.
There was one in grand equipage,
   Who was weeping as she rode
By the little House o' Happiness
   That's built beside the road.

When they have reached the lofty summit,
   And their dreams of greed come true,
Their souls are drained and empty,
   And their hearts are hardened, too,
And their worth is rather smaller
   Than the tiniest green-backed toad,
At the little House o' Happiness
   That's built beside the road.

Ah if they could only know it,
   As they push on through the strife,
'Tis the spirit of contentment
   That brings joy and peace in life.
Are you in that crowd beloved?
   Then come and cast aside your load—
Find the little House o' Happiness
   That's built beside the road.

THEY, TOO

(1917)

From the sunny South to the wind-swept North,
  All unmarked, forgotten, scattered,
Are the graves of the sleepers who have fared them forth
  And on the doors of Justice have battered.

If the cause was just and the time was ripe,
  What of swords, or spears, or guns?
For these were America's original type—
  They, too, would fight the Huns.

We know the history of the U. S. A.,
  And the men who have made it, too;
Some were the men who wore the gray
  And full many who wore the blue.

They may now be sleeping—our braves of old—
  And have been for many suns,
But could they assemble again so bold,
  They, too, would fight the Huns.

When the German arm with its grasping greed,
  Reached to encircle the globe,
It flung itself in Justice's face,
  And bloodied her snowwhite robe.

Columbia's laddies were strong and brave,
   And could shoulder many guns;
She knew that, Justice's face to save,
   They, too, must fight the Huns.

Up and down our peaceful, broad, fair land,
   From each little hamlet and town,
See! they come rushing with willing hand,
   To don the suits of brown.

"Get us all ready and you can just bet
   With lots of munitions and guns,
We won't forget Friend Lafayette;
   We, too, would fight the Huns."

And when they were landed on foreign shores,
   These khaki-clad lads so game,
It was "Over the top!" with whoops and roars—
   "We'll get 'em just the same."

Then fear came into the Hun beast's heart,
   When he saw the Yank and his guns,
For never had he even dreamed in part
   We, too, could fight the Huns.

The men of the Allies looked on in amaze,
   And questioned among each other:

"This wonderful spirit of these fighting lads,
　Where did they get it, my brother?"

Oh! Think of the sleepers of the long gone years,
　And how they shouldered their guns,
This is the spirit of our pioneers—
　They, too, would fight the Huns!

EVEN ONE

If I might write one poem,
  Or perchance a verse or two,
That would sink into the mem'ry
  Of my readers, ages through,
I would ask for inspiration
  And all my talents I would bend
Into paying lasting tribute
  To *one* true, unfaltering friend.

In your hours of meditation,
  Did you e'er by chance reflect
That an ordinary mortal
  So *few* blessings should expect?
But, if I had the choosing
  Of the highest Fate could send,
I'd just ask for the possession
  Of *one* firm, unfaltering friend.

The world is full of people
  Who may beam and smile on you,
But put them to one trying test,
  And not many will ring true.
But I know that 'mongst the thousands
  Of those faithless without end,
I have one who'll never fail me—
  I *have* one unfaltering friend.

And if at any gathering
　My chair vacant you should find,
I need feel no apprehension—
　I shall never be maligned.
For, staunch to fight for me my battles,
　Quick to praise or to defend,
I am ably represented
　By this same unfaltering friend.

Tho' my life has held much sunshine,
　I have had full mete of woes;
Tho' I've had the cheer of friendship,
　I have deeply felt my foes.
And when darkest hours found me—
　Ah! so few can comprehend
What a comfort and joy-bringer
　Was this dear, unfaltering friend.

I would not pray for riches,
　For fine mansions or for gold—
The most priceless of possessions
　Can be neither bought nor sold.
For the greatest of all blessings
　That a gen-rous Fate can send
Is the offering to a mortal
　Even one unfaltering friend.

And when my life is ended
And I meet my Lord above,
I am trusting Him to give me
Just *this* symbol of His love:
To let me find there, close beside Him,
In the light His face shall lend,
With the same old smile to greet me—
Just this *one* unfaltering friend.

MY JEWEL CASKET

I have a jewel casket
  Made of mellow, beaten gold,
And a tiny key that locks it;
  They are lovely to behold.
And within are priceless treasures
  Gathered through the years gone by—
I have gained them through much striving,
  And shall hold them till I die.

First, here lies my glittering diamonds,
  They are "Laughter," clear and fine,
Sunny smiles and tinkling cymbals,
  Life to your soul and to mine.
For a treasure house is barren
  If this jewel is not there;
It will keep your spirits youthful,
  And will mock at dull, gray care.

Then, my pearls so softly glowing,
  They're "Contentment" of the Soul—
Restful to the weary hearted,
  Lilies in a golden bowl.
And this jewel is the rarest,
  Meaning most to lives so bare;
I am sure that of all others
  These, my pearls, I least could spare.

Then this glorious sapphire pendant
    That is "Happiness" winging by,
Soaring joyously toward Heaven
    Like a Bluebird in the sky.
If we all could only capture
    Just a feather from its wing,
It would fill our lives with rapture
    And our hearts would ever sing.

Here's the changing opal earrings,
    They are "Sympathy," you'll find:
Ears that list to others' sorrows
    Earn the love of all mankind.
Listen to the man of wisdom,
    Listen to the song of woe,
And your sympathy will aid them
    As they, striving, onward go.

And these hand-wrought ruby bracelets,
    "Human Love" so warm and red,
Holding helpful hands, outstretching,
    Giving hungry wand'rers bread.
For your hands were meant for service,
    And there's much that they can do
Toward the lifting of the burdens
    Of those cumbered more than you.

Last, a circlet, this of moonstones,
    They are "Peace" so hardly won;
Quietly restful, soul deep-filling,
    May it last till time is done.
Peace, the circlet for the nations,
    May it be their choice full *wise*
Till all creation's war-slain millions
    On that Glorious Day shall rise.

Do you have a jewel casket
    Holding these and many more?
Do you revel in your treasures,
    Daily con them o'er and o'er?
Do you feel toward yours in fancy
    That to you these gems have brought
Higher aim and nobler purpose?—
    Then they were not vainly wrought!

WOODROW WILSON'S DAY

When, as an eager youngster, I used to read in books
Of all the world's great heroes and their deeds and fame and
    looks,
I'd glory in the courage of the men who led the fray
And pine because I, too, could not have lived in that good day.

I was thrilled by tales of Nero and of Caesar, I recall,
Of Hamilton and Bonaparte—such wondrous heroes all—
And I'd read and muse upon them, and shake my head and say,
"I wish that I'd been living in that good old stirring day."

I'd read American history—how they fought to be set free;
And the Revolution's leaders, almost immortal, seemed to me.
Why, those first American women fought the Indians, so
    they say;
I used to think I'd missed a lot by not living in that day.

Then, too, I'd hear Grandmother tell of the war that she'd
    lived thro',
Of Robert Lee and Davis, and what they sought to do,
And of her own husband falling at Vicksburg in the Gray—
I used to think there'd never be such doings in my day.

But, oh, the years did bring to pass such horrors as 'twould
    seem
Would rival any history or any youthful dream,

And I've seen such mortal courage that I never more can say,
"There were no noble heroes that lived within my day."

For: for cool deliberation and for utter *dauntlessness,*
I'll name you our leader, thro' this recent world-wide stress—
Not the hero of a nation, but of *all* the world, I say,
And I'm glad that I *was* living
                    In Woodrow Wilson's Day!

FAITH

Oh! sentinel oak on yonder hill,
    Mine eyes oft stray to thee;
I marvel at thy great gnarled strength,
    And wonder what you see
As, high above the other trees,
    You plume and dip and sway;
I think perhaps you're conning o'er
    The dreams of by-gone day.

How many years have you there been,
    How many seasons weathered;
How many song birds in your boughs
    Their little nests have feathered?
How many laborers, weary and worn,
    Have sought comfort in your shade;
How many lovers strolling there
    Their plighted troth have made?

My life at best can only be
    The promised three score ten,
But you, so firm on yonder hill,
    Mayhap a century's been;
You've seen the young grow old and die,
    And their young grow old again;
You've stood amidst the wearing years
    Of sleet and storm and rain.

Unruffled there in state you rise
　With no thought for the morrow,
Serene in Mother Nature's care
　You have no woe or sorrow.
With face uplifted to the sun
　And feet sunk 'neath the sod,
Your waving, graceful, swirling arms
　Waft praises up to God.

Oh! would that I were now as you,
　And as serenely met the morn
And bent my will to Nature's God
　From dusk until the dawn;
To stand erect in sunshine,
　And in storm to sway and nod,
To trust my life to Nature
　And to trust my soul to God.

DAHLIAS

To Emily White Lindsey

Just outside there in my garden,
    Lifting up their stately heads,
Are my regal rose-flamed dahlias,
    Gorgeous in their earthy beds.

Falling leaves are all about me,
    Autumn's knocking at my door,
But in their glowing, flaming beauty
    One forgets that Summer's o'er.

All my bridal wreath and pansies,
    Peonies, phlox and lilies fair,
All my daintiest fragile flowers
    Have vanished in the Summer air.

But you are here, my Compensation,
    In your graceful, lofty pride,
And I forget to mourn the blossoms
    That have withered by your side.

FAIRY FINGERS

O, Fairy Fingers on my brow,
　　So cool and soft and light
They banish care from my dull brain
　　As daybreak scatters night.
Their touch some magic seems to hold
　　So deep and dear and sweet,
I yield my being up to yours
　　And kneel me at your feet.

O, Fairy Fingers on the keys,
　　Your music fills my soul;
It gathers up my broken life
　　And mends it, makes it whole.
Your touch so rare but seems to me
　　Like twinkling, fairy wings;
The harp you play is half divine—
　　It seems to me it sings.

O, Fairy Fingers through my hair
　　As drowsing here I sit
At twilight hour, in firelight glow,
　　The lamps as yet unlit.
I feel their warmth steal to my heart
　　And raise my hands to hold them,
Then kiss each dainty fragrant tip
　　(Like rose leaves you unfold them.)

O, Fairy Fingers cross my eyes,
  I pray you leave me never,
But when life's journey ends for me
  And the silver cord I sever,
Press gently on my quiet lids
  (And do not weep o'ermuch)
For I will then so sweetly sleep
  When lulled by your dear touch.

Index

Index
(*Continued*)